First Aid & Home Safety

Tony Napoli

A LifeSchool™ Work Text

Fearon Education
a division of
David S. Lake Publishers
Belmont, California

Copyright © 1985 by David S. Lake Publishers, 19 Davis Drive, Belmont, CA 94002. All rights reserved. No part of this book may be reproduced by any means, transmitted, or translated into a machine language without written permission from the publisher.

ISBN-0-8224-4366-X

Printed in the United States of America

1.9 8 7 6 5 4 3

Contents

	Introduction	1
1	Wounds	3
2	Shock	10
3	Respiratory Emergencies	15
4	Poisonings	22
5	Burns	29
6	Weather Injuries	36
7	Fire in the Home	42
8	Electricity and Gas in the Home	50
	Posttest	57
	Answers to Exercises	59

Introduction

Have you ever seen someone suddenly become very ill and not known what you could do to help? Have you ever driven by an accident that just happened and not known how to help those who were hurt? Have you ever hurt *yourself* so badly that you became frightened and couldn't think clearly enough to help yourself?

Well, this happens to many, many people all the time. Most people in good health never stop to think of what may happen in a *health emergency*. All they know to do is to go to the nearest doctor or hospital.

But sometimes doctors and hospitals are far away. And if something happens that needs care *right away*, you may not have enough time to travel for help. Lives have been lost because people waited too long before reaching a hospital or doctor for care.

That is why knowing first aid can be so valuable. It allows you to help someone who is sick or hurt *during the time* it may take to get to a hospital or doctor.

The first six chapters in this book will teach you some simple first aid steps. You will not learn so much that you will be able to do what a person trained in medicine for years can do. But you will learn how to quickly help someone who is in pain from a bad injury. And you will be able to help someone who is frightened because he or she has suddenly become very ill and doesn't know why or what to do. And one day, what you have learned may even save someone's life.

The final two chapters in this book are about another valuable subject—home safety. Many of the accidents that take place around the home each year do not have to happen. All it takes is knowing what you have in your home that can be dangerous—and then learning the best ways to be careful with these things. The chapters on home safety will tell you that—and more.

Reading this book will not make you a doctor or an expert on home safety. But it will help you deal with health problems that happen to millions of people every day. And it will tell you about all the useful—but dangerous—things we have around the home. For these reasons this book can be valuable to you—now and in the years ahead.

Chapter 1
Wounds

Lubbock Tribune
Search Still on for Mad Bus Wrecker

SHERIDAN, TEXAS—Police here are still looking for a car they are calling the "mad bus wrecker" of Sheridan County. They have stepped up their search after the third bus-car accident in a week happened on Monday. Police say they are certain all three crashes were caused by the same person or persons driving the same car.

Witnesses have described the car as a bright red late 1960s Chevy with a loud race car motor. They also have told police that the car's front doors have pictures of a bus with a skull with crossbones on top of it and the words "NOT SAFE" written underneath.

Passengers who were riding on the three buses have all told police the same story. Each time the red Chevy, traveling at high speed, suddenly cuts in front of the bus. The driver is either forced to jam on the brakes or swerve sharply to avoid hitting the red car.

In the first two accidents, the driver jammed his brakes so quickly that the bus was rammed hard from behind. Several passengers and the drivers of the cars all suffered minor injuries.

In Monday's accident on Interstate 14 the passengers were not as lucky. The bus driver, Jack Kramden, tried hard to avoid getting hit by cars behind him. When he did so, the bus skidded off the road and overturned in a ditch 15 feet below the highway.

Five passengers were cut badly by broken glass and one suffered a broken leg. Kramden, the driver, was pinned inside for nearly an hour and suffered internal injuries. They were all taken to Norton General Hospital for treatment. Paramedics treated several other passengers at the scene for minor scrapes and bruises.

Police say they are talking with officials of the Sheridan Transit Company which owns and runs the bus line. They are trying to find out if any ex-employees at Sheridan Transit may be holding a grudge against the company.

Words to Learn

treatment the care or medicine given to someone who is ill

Thousands of car accidents occur every day across the United States. They happen so often that only the unusual or very serious ones are still reported in the newspapers. Many of these accidents take place miles from the nearest hospital or doctor. The people in these accidents sometimes need medical help right away at the scene.

Suppose you happened upon that bus accident in the news story. Or suppose you had been in the accident yourself. How would you help the people who had been badly cut? How could you help the driver who had internal injuries? And would you know the signs of a broken leg?

The first few minutes after an accident or injury are very important. Good first aid **treatment** often must be given before a doctor arrives. If you know how to help an injured person, it can sometimes mean the difference between life and death.

Words to Learn

rescue to save a person from danger

The Best Way to Help

If possible get help to **rescue** a victim. If you try to do it alone and are not careful you may breathe in too much of the poison and become trapped like the victim.

Before entering a closed room or garage filled with gas or smoke take a deep breath and hold it. Try to get as close to the ground as possible so you will not breathe the gas. Pull the victim out into fresh air. If that is not possible, let fresh air into the room.

Loosen any tight clothing around the victim's neck and waist. Give the victim mouth-to-mouth breathing if needed. Call for help from a hospital as soon as possible. Tell the hospital that oxygen will be needed. Do this even if the victim seems to be much better after being removed from the area.

Exercises

Darken the circles next to each right answer.

1. Which of the following are signs that a person may have swallowed a poison?
   ○ burns around the lips and mouth
   ○ high fever
   ○ weak pulse
   ○ strong breath odor

2. Some *general* first aid steps you can take for a poisoning victim are _____ .
   ○ dilute the poison
   ○ give the victim fluids
   ○ keep the person breathing
   ○ get help from a Poison Control Center

3. The best ways to get a poisoning victim to vomit are _____ .
   ○ give the person fruit juices
   ○ place your finger in the back of the victim's throat
   ○ give the person Syrup of Ipecac
   ○ hold the person upside-down

4. Which of the following poisons usually should not be vomited?
   ○ bleach
   ○ weed killer
   ○ glue
   ○ liquid cleaner
   ○ lighter fluid

5. Which of the following steps should be taken with an *unconscious* poisoning victim?
   ○ loosen any tight clothing around the neck and waist
   ○ give fluids to dilute the poison
   ○ clear an airway for mouth-to-mouth breathing
   ○ get the victim to vomit the poison

6. Which of the following are first aid steps for a poison gas or smoke victim?
   ○ pull the victim out into fresh air
   ○ cut off the source of the gas or smoke
   ○ give the victim mouth-to-mouth breathing
   ○ give the victim fluids

Words to Remember

condition	dilute	liquid	rescue
convulsions	dizzy	odor	

Chapter 5
Burns

Grantville Times
Mummy Has a Really Scary Halloween

DETROIT—One minute Ann Rains was laughing and enjoying herself at a friend's Halloween party. The next minute a careless smoker brushed up against her and set her mummy costume on fire.

This morning she is in Chaney Hospital's burn center, lucky to be alive. Ms. Rains suffered second-degree burns on her hands, chest, back, and legs.

Ms. Rains had wanted to look like the mummy from those old horror movies. So she made her costume out of gauze and cotton balls. And she *did* look the part. But her costume was also dangerous. Its materials can easily catch on fire.

And that's just what happened. But two of her friends knew just what to do. One of them grabbed a blanket and smothered the flames. Then they both wrapped her in water-soaked sheets until the hospital emergency unit arrived.

"The doctors told me it could have been much worse," Ms. Rains said this morning. "They said even another half minute and I could have had third-degree burns over more than half of my body. It's a good thing my friends acted quickly," she said.

Asked if she has given up on Halloween costumes, Ms. Rains said, "No, not at all. But," she added, "next year I think I'll dress up in something safe—like a suit of armor."

Helping a burn victim who is on fire can be a life-saving first aid measure. Sometimes, as with Ann Rains, it can mean the difference between bad burns in a few places and major burns all over the body.

Burn injuries often happen when people are not being careful. We never think twice about lying in the sun, lighting matches, washing with cleaners and detergents, or just using electricity. So we forget that we are dealing with things that can be dangerous. That's when a burn accident takes place. And that's when we need to know first aid for burns.

Heat Burns

A burn injury can be caused by many things. Burns are *classified*—or grouped—by what causes them and how badly they hurt the victim.

Burns that are caused by fire, sunlight, or any hot matter can be called heat burns. They are grouped by **degree**—first, second, or third. First-degree burns are the least dangerous; third-degree burns are the most dangerous.

First-Degree Burns

Causes and Signs

A first-degree burn causes damage only to the outside **layer** of skin. Sunburn or touching something hot for a few seconds are the most common causes of this kind of burn.

The signs of a first-degree burn are redness; some pain and swelling; and unbroken skin (no **blisters**).

Words to Learn

degree   one of a number of steps or stages

layer   one of several levels of thickness of something

blister   watery, bubble-shaped swelling of the skin

The Best Way to Help

Quickly place the burn under cold running water. Or, put on a cold-water compress such as a clean towel or washcloth. Do this until the pain lets up. Then cover the burn with a clean bandage.

Don't Do This

1. Do not put butter or grease on the burn.

2. Do not put any other medicines on the burn without a doctor's OK.

Second-Degree Burns

Causes and Signs

A second-degree burn causes damage to the layers of the skin beneath the body surface. Deep sunburn, touching hot liquids, or a flash burn from something like gasoline, are causes of second-degree burns.

The symptoms of second-degree burns are redness or a spotty look to the burn; blisters; swelling that lasts for days; a wet feel to the skin; or pain.

The Best Way to Help

Place the burn under cold water or put on a cold compress until the pain lets up. Gently pat the burn dry with something clean and soft. Then cover the burn with a clean bandage. If an arm or leg has been burned, raise it above the heart.

A victim with fire burns around the lips or mouth may have trouble breathing. In that case, get medical attention right away at a hospital.

Don't Do This

1. Do not try to break blisters.

2. Do not put on any medicines without a doctor's OK.

> **Special Note**
>
> Get quick medical attention for any person who has been burned on over 15 percent of the body (10 percent for a child). A good way to judge is to figure that a hand makes up about one percent of the body. Also seek medical help for anyone with bad burns of the hands, face, or feet.

Third-Degree Burns

Causes and Signs

A third-degree burn destroys all layers of a person's skin. Fire and electrical burns can often be the causes of third-degree burns.

The signs of a third-degree burn are the burn is white or charred, the skin is destroyed and there is not much pain because the nerve endings have been destroyed.

The Best Way to Help

Any person with even small third-degree burns needs medical attention. Call for emergency help quickly. Take the following first aid steps: If the victim is on fire, wrap the person in a blanket or bedspread. This should put out the flames. Give mouth-to-mouth breathing if needed. Cool any burns of the face, feet or hands with cool water or a cold compress. Cover the burn area with a thick, clean dressing such as a sheet or pillowcase.

NOTE: *Third-degree burn victims often go into shock. First aid treatment for shock is described in Chapter 2.*

Don't Do This

1. Do not remove clothes that stick to the burn.
2. Do not put ice or ice water on the burn.
3. Do not put any medicines on the burn without a doctor's OK.
4. Do not give fluids to a victim who is unconscious, having convulsions or may need surgery.
5. Do not give alcohol to any victim.

Chemical Burns of the Skin

Dangerous chemicals and poisons that get on the skin may cause very bad burns. They must be washed quickly before they do serious damage to the skin and tissues.

The Best Way to Help

Wash the burned area with running water for at least five minutes. Use a hose or shower or tub if possible. Try not to use a strong stream of water. While washing, remove the victim's clothing from the burn area. Follow any first aid directions which may be on the label of the chemical. Apply a cool, wet bandage to ease the pain. Get medical help as soon as possible.

Eye Burns

Eye burns from such things as bleach, liquid cleaners, and detergents can be very dangerous. If the eye is not washed and treated very quickly, the victim could become blind.

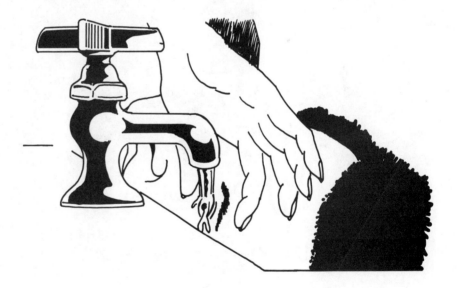

The Best Way to Help

Before calling medical help, wash the eye with large amounts of cool running water. Place the victim's head under a faucet with the eyelid held open. Let the water run from the inside corner of the eye (next to the nose) outward for about ten minutes. This way the water will run off the face and not get the chemical into the other eye. If both eyes have been burned, let the water flow over both. Make sure all parts of the eye are thoroughly washed.

After washing, cover the eye with a clean cloth and put a bandage in place. Close the eye before bandaging. Get medical help from an eye doctor as soon as possible.

Don't Do This

Do not let the victim rub the burned eye.

Exercises

Read each question. Then write your answers on the lines below.

1. Heat burns are grouped by degree—first, second, and third. Which is the most dangerous?
   _____
   _____

2. What are the two basic first aid steps for treating a first-degree burn?
   _____
   _____

3. Name three common causes of a second-degree burn.
   _____
   _____
   _____

4. Quick medical attention is needed for any victim with burns over how much of the body?
   _____
   _____

5. What are the symptoms of a third-degree burn?
   _____
   _____

6. Third-degree burns are very dangerous. What often happens to victims with this kind of burn?
   _____
   _____

7. What kind of treatment do you use for a chemical burn of the skin?
   _____
   _____

8. When you wash an eye burn, you should run the water *outward* off the face. Why?
   _____
   _____

Words to Remember

blister   degree   layer

Chapter 6
Weather Injuries

One night, Grace Porter and her cousin Bill Miller were driving home from the ice-skating rink. Suddenly the car began to shake and sputter. In a moment the engine began to rattle, and then it just stopped.

"What happened?" Bill asked.

"I don't know," Grace said. She tried to start the engine again. Nothing happened.

"Well, now what?" Bill said. He looked out the window. It was dark and cold outside. And the road was empty. "We're in the middle of nowhere," he said.

"We have to find a phone and call the auto club," said Grace. "Let's get going," she said.

An hour later Grace and Bill were still walking. They hadn't seen one house and not a single car had driven by.

"How are you doing?" Grace asked her cousin.

"OK, I guess," Bill answered. "I sure wish I had worn gloves and some warmer shoes though," he said.

Soon they saw lights, and smoke coming from a chimney.

"Hey, finally a house!" Bill shouted.

When they reached the door a woman came out to

meet them. Bill and Grace explained what happened to their car and the woman let them inside to phone for help.

"You kids look frozen," the woman said. "Let me make you some hot tea. My name is Kathy Wilson."

While Grace called the auto club, Bill walked over to a radiator and put his hands on top of it.

When Mrs. Wilson came back into the living room, Grace had gotten off the phone. "The auto club said someone would be here within the hour," Grace said.

"Well, you can stay warm in here," Mrs. Wilson said. She gave Grace some tea. "Here, drink this," she said.

Bill was still standing at the radiator. "I can't feel my hands and feet," he said. "I hope they warm up soon."

Mrs. Wilson walked over to him. She looked at his hands and became worried. "Your fingers are very white and ice-cold," she said. She squeezed Bill's fingers hard. "Can you feel that?" she asked.

"No, I can't feel anything," Bill said.

"I'm afraid you may have frostbite," Mrs. Wilson said. "You better take your hands and feet away from the radiator. You could burn them without knowing it."

"Frostbite!" Grace said. "That's bad, isn't it?" she asked. "Shouldn't we get some hot water?"

"Yes, we can heat some water right away," Mrs. Wilson said. "It shouldn't be too hot, though. Come into the kitchen, Bill. It's a good thing we noticed your condition early. It could have gotten a lot worse if you'd had to walk much farther."

Words to Learn

exhaustion   feeling very, very tired and weak

Without even knowing it Bill Miller had badly injured himself. One of the real dangers of frostbite is that very often victims don't even know they have it. Usually their bodies are so cold that they don't realize they have lost all feeling in their toes, fingers, or ears. That's because those body parts have been in the cold for so long they have become frozen.

People get frostbite from being out in very cold weather for too long. Being out in very *hot* weather for too long can also be very dangerous. It can lead to heatstroke or heat **exhaustion.** All of these conditions can be very serious if they are not treated quickly. And all of them *can* be treated quickly by knowing the right first aid steps to take.

Words to Learn

numb without any feeling

rewarm to make warm again

thawed melted or unfrozen

Frostbite

When someone stays out in very cold weather for too long that person can get frostbite. Frostbite simply means that parts of your body have frozen. It mostly attacks the nose, fingers, ears, toes, or cheeks. Many times the victim does not even know that he or she has frostbite. That makes it even more dangerous. If frostbite is not treated it can lead to shock and cause death.

Signs

The symptoms of frostbite become worse as time passes. At first, the skin is red and there is some pain. Then the skin becomes white or a gray-yellow. The skin feels firm and like wax. There may be blisters. The pain goes away, but the skin becomes very cold and **numb**. Frostbite victims often do not know they are hurt until someone else notices the way their skin looks.

The Best Way to Help

There are several first aid steps you can take for frostbite. In helping the victim you have two goals. One is to warm all frozen parts quickly. The second is to protect those parts from further damage.

First, cover all frozen parts with extra clothing or blankets. Put frostbitten hands or fingers under the victim's armpits for extra warmth. Bring the victim inside as quickly as possible. **Rewarm** the frozen parts by putting them in *warm* water. The water temperature should be between 100 and 104° Fahrenheit. Test the water temperature either with a thermometer or by pouring it on the inside of your arm.

NOTE: If the frozen part has **thawed** and then refrozen, warm it at around room temperature: 70 to 74° Fahrenheit.

If water can't be used, gently wrap the frozen parts in blankets or other warm things. Separate frozen toes or fingers by putting dry gauze between them. Raise any frozen parts so that they are above the heart if possible.

Stop any warming once the skin becomes pink or when the person gets some feeling back. Once feeling has returned, have the victim stretch and move any frozen part. Get medical help as soon as possible.

Don't Do This

1. Do not *rub* any frozen part; it may make the condition worse.

Words to Learn

immediately at once; now
confused not thinking clearly

2. Do not use heat lamps, hot-water bottles, or heating pads to warm frozen parts.
3. Do not break any blisters.
4. Do not let the victim place any frozen parts on a radiator or a hot stove.
5. Do not give the victim any alcoholic drinks. Give warm liquids such as tea, coffee, or soup.
6. Do not let any victim with frozen toes or feet walk.

Heatstroke

Heatstroke is caused when a person's body gets too much heat for a long period of time. Heatstroke is a very serious condition. First aid must be used **immediately** to cool the body.

Signs

The following signs are symptoms of heatstroke: The body temperature is very high—106° Fahrenheit or more. The skin is hot, red, and dry. There is no sweating. The pulse is strong and fast. The victim may be **confused** or unconscious.

The Best Way to Help

If the person's body temperature reaches 105° Fahrenheit or higher, take the following steps: Undress the victim and place the person in a tub of cold (*not iced*) water. If that is not possible, use a sponge with cold water or rubbing alcohol to cool off the victim. Or, you can use cold towels or washcloths to do this.

If they are available, use fans or air conditioners to cool off the victim. Continue cooling until the victim's body

temperature goes down to 101 to 102° Fahrenheit. If the victim has been cooled in a tub, make sure you dry the person off completely. If the body temperature begins to rise again, repeat the cooling treatment. In any case, get medical help as soon as possible.

Don't Do This

Do not give the victim any alcohol or other fluids.

Heat Exhaustion

Heat exhaustion happens when too much heat causes someone to become so tired and weak that he or she cannot move.

Signs

A person suffering from heat exhaustion will show the following signs: The body temperature is normal or just above normal. The skin is pale and sticky. The victim is very tired, weak, and sweating a lot. The victim might have a headache, cramps, and dizziness. The victim may vomit and even pass out.

The Best Way to Help

Move the victim to a cooler place. Have the victim lie down. Raise the feet up 8 to 12 inches. Loosen any tight clothing around the neck and waist. Place cool and wet cloth on the body.

If the victim is not vomiting you can give fluids. Mix one teaspoon of salt for every glass of cool water. Give the victim half a glass every 15 minutes for up to an hour. Stop giving water if the victim vomits. If the symptoms become worse or last for more than an hour get medical attention.

Special Note

A victim with heat exhaustion may sometimes get *heat cramps*. The muscles in the legs and abdomen will become very tight and begin to hurt. To treat this, put pressure with your hands on any cramped muscles to loosen them. Or, you can gently massage them to ease the pain.

Exercises

Darken the circle next to the right answer.

1. Frostbite is a condition where parts of the body _____ .
   - ○ become soft
   - ○ become very warm
   - ○ become frozen
   - ○ fall off

Darken the circle next to each right answer.

2. Which of the following are symptoms of frostbite?
   - ○ white, firm skin
   - ○ high fever
   - ○ crying a lot
   - ○ bad headaches
   - ○ very cold, numb skin

Darken the circle next to the right answer.

3. The temperature of the water used to rewarm frostbitten body parts should be _____ .
   - ○ around 98.6° Fahrenheit
   - ○ 100° Fahrenheit
   - ○ no higher than 104° Fahrenheit
   - ○ 106° Fahrenheit

4. The condition caused by a person getting too much heat for a long time is called _____ .
   - ○ sunburn
   - ○ heatstroke
   - ○ frostbite
   - ○ heat exhaustion

5. The most important first aid step in treating heatstroke is to _____ .
   - ○ get the victim to lie down
   - ○ get the victim something to eat
   - ○ get the victim something to drink
   - ○ cool the victim's body immediately

6. The big difference between heatstroke and heat exhaustion is that a victim with heat exhaustion _____ .
   - ○ has a normal or slightly higher body temperature and sweats a lot
   - ○ is always unconscious
   - ○ falls asleep quickly
   - ○ takes a lot longer to get well

7. The best liquid to give a victim with heat exhaustion is _____ .
   - ○ fruit juice
   - ○ coffee
   - ○ soda
   - ○ cool water mixed with salt

Words to Remember

confused	immediately	rewarm	thawed
exhaustion	numb		

Chapter 7
Fire in the Home

One warm and sunny Sunday afternoon Bob Hartley went out to his backyard. Then he called to his girlfriend Suzanne Ashley, "It's such a beautiful day. Why don't we have a barbecue?"

"That sounds great," Suzanne said. "Do you have any steaks or chicken to cook?"

"There should be a couple of steaks in the refrigerator. Why don't you prepare them and I'll get the grill."

Fifteen minutes later Bob had set everything up. Suzanne carried out a tray with two juicy steaks ready to be cooked.

"I'm very low on lighter fluid," Bob said. "But I think I have enough to get the fire going."

Bob started the fire and put the steaks on the grill. A few minutes later the fire began to go out.

"Oh no, the fire is running down," he said. "And I used the last of the lighter fluid."

"I can run down to the market and get some more," Suzanne said.

"Wait a minute. I have some extra gasoline in a can out

back here," Bob said. "I can just use that to restart the fire."

"Are you crazy?" Suzanne shouted. "Do you want to cause an explosion? Don't you know you should never use gasoline to start a charcoal fire? You use only charcoal lighter fluid."

"I thought I could use only a little bit just to restart it," Bob said. "There's plenty of lighter fluid in there already."

"That's the point," Suzanne said. "The vapors from the gasoline could ignite and you could have an explosion and a fire."

"I didn't realize that," Bob said. "I guess we'd have some really 'well done' steaks, huh?"

"And I'd have a badly hurt boyfriend to go with them," Suzanne said. "Stay away from that fire with that gasoline. I'll be back in ten minutes with more lighter fluid."

> **Words to Learn**
>
> **explosion** when something blows up
> **hazards** dangers

Suzanne was right. If Bob had poured gasoline on the fire he would have caused an **explosion** and a fire. And he would have been very badly burned at the same time.

Bob was being very careless with gasoline—one of the most dangerous liquids we use. People like Bob start fires by accident every day. Many of them are not lucky enough to have someone nearby to stop them. The best way to prevent a fire accident is to learn as much as you can about all the things that cause them.

Fire! It is one of our country's most serious health dangers. Nearly 7,500 people die and another 300,000 are injured each year by fires. Fires also destroy more property each year than all natural disasters combined. And most of these fires start by accidents—accidents that could have been prevented.

Many fires are caused because people are careless. Many lives are lost and property is destroyed because people are not prepared once a fire does break out. The best way to prevent fires is to know all about the **hazards** that can cause them. The best way to save lives is to know just what to do when a fire does break out.

Words to Learn

ignited started on fire

flammable something that can catch on fire easily and burn quickly

fabric cloth

Fire Hazards

Fires can be caused by many things. They can be **ignited**—started—by matches, lighters, pilot lights, or overloaded electrical cords. When someone is careless with something **flammable**—liquid or **fabric**—the result is a fire accident. And many people are careless because they do not know enough about all the flammable things they have around the home. Learning about flammable things is the best way to *stop* a fire before it ever starts.

Flammable Liquids

Have you ever seen a person smoking while using nail polish remover or paint thinner? Do you know someone who stores an extra can of gasoline in the car trunk? Or, maybe you have noticed some cleaning fluids in a friend's garage stored near the pilot light of a gas heater?

People who do any of these things can easily cause a fire. They are being careless around flammable liquids. Most people know that flammable liquids will burn if exposed to a flame. But many people do not know how *fast* and how *easily* these liquids can and do burn.

Gasoline is one of the most dangerous of these liquids. Everyone knows what happens if you throw a match into some gasoline. But many people don't know that just the vapors from gasoline are dangerous. Vapors are gases and can't be seen. Gasoline vapors from an open can could move along the ground and be ignited by a flame or spark many feet away. The result will be an explosion and fire. And very bad burns for anyone nearby.

There are ways of preventing a fire with flammable liquids from ever starting. The best way to do this is to follow certain rules in using and storing these liquids.

Use

1. Never use a flammable liquid near an open flame. This includes "hidden" flames such as pilot lights of stoves, furnaces, and heaters.

2. Always use a flammable liquid out-of-doors or someplace that gets a lot of air.

3. Do not put gasoline in a gasoline-powered engine while it is running or still hot. Let it cool off before adding more fuel.

4. Do not start a charcoal fire with gasoline. Use only fuel labeled as a charcoal starter. Do not add more fuel to the fire once it has started. The flames could travel up to the can and cause an explosion.

Storage

1. Always store flammable liquids in a place that gets a lot of air. Keep them away from any open flame.

2. Store flammable liquids in safety cans with tight caps. Never store them in glass bottles or containers.

3. Keep flammable liquids locked up when you're not using them. Keep them out of the reach of children.

4. Don't store gasoline in the trunk of your car or in your home. If you need to store it, keep it away from where you live. Always keep gasoline in a special approved safety can.

Many people need to use some kind of flammable liquid in their everyday lives. Almost all such liquids have directions for use and care right on the label. It takes only a few minutes to read them. Any time you use a flammable liquid, read those directions on the can. And remember the safety rules listed above. They can help prevent a serious fire accident. And they can save your life as well.

Flammable Fabrics

Flammable liquids are not the only fire hazards we have in our homes. Many fires are caused when clothing or furniture begins to burn. Such fires can spread very quickly if the clothing or furniture is made of very flammable fabrics. It is important to know which of the fabrics that you own are flammable. This way you can reduce the chances of a fabric fire from ever starting in your home.

All fabrics burn. But some burn more easily than others. It depends on the kind of material used and how the object was made.

Clothing

The safest clothing to buy is that made with *flame resistant* fabrics. Flame resistant does not mean that these fabrics will not burn. It just means that they are better in resisting—or fighting off—flames than other fabrics.

Today most sleepwear clothing is made of flame resistant fabrics. This is especially true of sleepwear for children.

Words to Learn

garments something to wear; clothing

upholstery covering for furniture

Laws have been passed stating that sleepwear for *young* children *must* be flame resistant.

Flame resistant **garments** have labels that state this fact. The labels give certain rules for washing these garments. Special care must be taken so that certain soaps do not wash out the flame resistant chemical. Read all labels on these garments carefully before washing them.

When buying non-flame resistant clothing it is helpful to remember certain things. Fabrics that are light and loosely woven burn more easily than heavy, tightly woven ones. So, most cotton shirts will burn much faster than denim jeans.

Clothing made to fit loosely can easily catch on fire. Robes or housecoats with loose sleeves, long gowns, or hanging shirttails should never be worn near an open flame. Never cook near an open flame while wearing a loose-fitting garment.

Things Around the Home

Many things we have around the home can also catch on fire easily. Most furniture coverings—**upholstery**—are made of flammable fabrics. Bed mattresses, window drapes, carpets, and rugs are just some of the many other household things made with flammable fabrics.

The great danger from mattress and furniture fires is not always in getting burned. Most injuries and deaths from these fires are caused by breathing in smoke and poison gases. Often people sleep right through the early stages of a fire. By the time they awake there is enough smoke in the house to make them unconscious and cause death.

The greatest danger from mattress and furniture fires is breathing in smoke and poison gases.

Fire in the Home 47

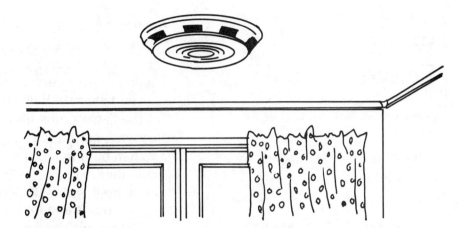

A *smoke detector* is a fire alarm that buzzes when it picks up smoke in a room. It is wise to put one on the ceiling on every level of your house, near bedrooms.

Words to Learn

panic   to become frightened

Be Careful

There are several steps you can take to guard against fabric fires in the home.

1. When buying furniture ask about the flammability of the fabric. Read the labels. Some furniture fabrics are more fire resistant than others.

2. Place all upholstered furniture far away from any open flame or heaters.

3. Check electric cords near upholstered furniture. Replace any worn-out cords.

4. If there are smokers in your house always be alert for dropped cigarettes or ashes. When someone has been smoking always check behind couch cushions and on carpets for smoke, ashes, or sparks.

5. Urge all smokers in your house *never* to smoke in bed or when otherwise sleepy. Most upholstered furniture and mattress fires are caused by victims who have fallen asleep while smoking.

If a Fire Breaks Out...

No matter how careful we are, an accidental fire sometimes happens. It can be a very frightening thing. Many people **panic** and become confused during a fire. That is why it is best to have a *plan of escape* from your house set up ahead of time. This way you will know exactly what to do to get out and get help as quickly as possible.

Escape Plan

1. Plan two exits from each room. Keep a rope or chain ladder in any second story room.

2. Choose a place to meet outside. This way you can tell if everyone has escaped.

3. If a fire breaks out, *get out fast*. Don't stop to take anything with you.

4. When leaving the house, keep low. Crawl on your hands and knees to avoid breathing in smoke. More people die from smoke in fires than from burns.

5. Before entering a closed room, touch the door *first*. If it feels hot don't enter. Call for help from a window.

6. Have a fire drill every so often. Practice your escape plan so that everyone will remember what to do in case of a fire.

These few simple steps can help save the lives of everyone in your house. They can also allow you to get help quickly and perhaps save your property as well.

Remember—learning more about the hazards we have at home can help prevent a fire from breaking out. Learning what to do when a fire does break out can help save your life.

Exercises

Read each question. Then write your answers on the lines below.

1. Name the four things that can ignite a fire.

   _____
   _____
   _____
   _____

2. What are three flammable liquids?

   _____
   _____
   _____

Read each statement. Then write "True" if the statement is true, or "False" if the statement is false.

3. Never use a flammable liquid near an open flame.

   _____

4. Once a gasoline-powered engine is running, you should then add more fuel to fill it up.

   _____

5. Always store flammable liquids in glass bottles or containers.

   _____

6. Flame resistant fabrics are fabrics that will never burn.

   _____

7. Most injuries and deaths from mattress and furniture fires are caused by breathing in smoke and poison gases.

   _____

8. As part of an escape plan in case of a fire, it is wise to keep a rope or chain ladder in any second story room.

   _____

Words to Remember

explosion	flammable	hazards	panic
fabric	garments	ignited	upholstery

Chapter 8
Electricity and Gas in the Home

Ellinburg Herald
Block Party was a Real "Blow-out"

COMSTOCK—The power blackout that lasted all day Sunday was caused by people at a Saturday night block party in the north end of the city, it was learned yesterday.

Officials of Comstock Power and Light said the power drain at their north central station was too great for their system. "We had a bad overload at around 1 a.m. and our system just shut down," company spokesperson Joan Grant said.

"When the system is overloaded the safety features shut it down so we won't have a fire," Ms. Grant said. "In this case we lost power to most of the north and central parts of the city."

Yesterday the company was able to locate the reason for the power failure. It learned that people

Electricity and Gas in the Home 51

living on Tracy Drive had a block party Saturday night.

"The people on the block had far too many electrical things going at once," Ms. Grant said. "We found out that they had air conditioners running inside while they were cooking with electric stoves and grills outside. They had bands with electric guitars playing and party lights strung all along the street," she said.

"These people just created a mess," she added in an angry voice. "It was as if they never even thought about all the electricity they were using."

Grant went on to warn city residents planning the same kind of party. "If you plan a block party, be careful with the electrical things you use. Don't overload the systems of the homes on your block. Otherwise we may have more blackouts like this one," she said.

The company said that power was back on all over the city by early yesterday morning.

Two of the most useful sources of energy we have are electricity and gas. Much of our daily lives depends on these two kinds of power. But electricity and gas can also be very dangerous. Thousands of accidents happen each year because people—like those in Comstock—are careless. The best way to prevent such accidents is to learn all about the hazards of using electricity and gas.

Words to Learn

system   a group of things working together to make something run

capacity   the largest amount that something can take

electrician   a person who makes a living working with electrical things

Electricity in the Home

There are two major dangers when using electricity—fire and shock. Accidents that cause either of these two things can badly hurt and even kill a person. Today we know so much about how electricity works that nearly all such accidents can be prevented. The first step is to learn all about the electricity in your home.

Many people do not know enough about how the electricity in their home works. All they know is that if they plug in a lamp or toaster and turn it on, it should work. An important fact people overlook is that their homes can only handle a certain *load* of power. If they use too many electrical things, they can *overload* their electrical **system**. And that's how a fire can start very quickly.

You should learn how much **capacity** your electrical system has. That simply means how many electric things you can use at the same time without overloading. In many places, you can learn this from your local power company. If you ask, they will send someone out to your house to explain your system to you. Usually this is done free of charge. In some places you may have to call an **electrician** and pay for the service.

In either case you can learn all the important things you need to know. These include the following: How much load can your system take? Is the system out-of-date? Is some of the wiring worn and in need of replacement? What kind of safety features does the system have? These questions and others can be answered by your power company or an electrician.

Using Your System Safely

Once you have learned about your electrical system, you need to do two things. You have to make sure it works well for you. And you have to make sure that you always use it safely.

Don't Overload

Once you know the capacity of your system, don't use more electricity than it can take. Learn which of your electrical things use the most power. For example, toasters, irons, and hair dryers use much more power than lamps, radios, and can openers. Try not to have too many major power-users on at the same time. You can learn all about the electric things you own from the information books that come with them.

Electricity and Gas in the Home 53

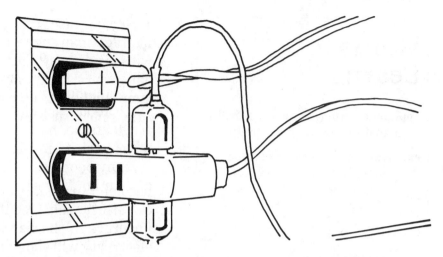

Don't overload wall outlets with too many cords or plugs. They can cause a fire.

Most systems have safety features to guard against a fire that might be caused by overloading. Some systems "blow" fuses. Others "open" circuit breakers. In both cases the result is the same. Power to a part of the house is cut off. You then have to replace a fuse or "flip" the circuit breaker to get power back. If you're not sure which system you have, call the power company or an electrician.

Remember—even with safety features, overloading is dangerous. An electrical fire can still start because the safety features may not be working properly. And you wouldn't know this until it was too late.

Use Proper Fuses and Lightbulbs

Many people don't know enough about fuses. Fuses are rated by *amperes*, which is a term for measuring electricity. Most home fuses are rated at 15, 20, 25, or 30 amperes. Using a 30-ampere fuse when you should only use a 15-ampere fuse can be *very* dangerous. The electricity will keep on flowing and that can cause a serious electrical fire.

Most fuse boxes *do not* tell you what size fuse you should use. As a rule, most homes older than 25 years can only take a certain number of 15-ampere fuses. Homes built since the 1960s can take fuses higher than that. If you're not sure about your fuse box, call a trained person to help you. Once again, someone from the local power company can tell you.

Many people put lightbulbs in their lamps and ceiling lights without thinking much about it. But most lamps and lights can only take lightbulbs of a certain *wattage* (power). Many lamps and lights tell you what kind of lightbulbs to use. It is written right on them. They will say "Use 60-watt bulbs"— or 75 or 100.

> **Words to Learn**
>
> **appliances** things used in a home or office that run by gas or electricity
>
> **extension cords** electrical cords that can connect with another cord to reach a wall outlet

In most cases this means you can use lightbulbs with *less* wattage than suggested. But you should never use any with higher wattage. Using a wattage that is too high is dangerous. It can cause overheating and lead to a fire. If your lamps and lights do not suggest certain lightbulbs, a good rule is not to use any above 60 watts.

Fix Bad Wiring

Over the years, the cords on your electrical things may become worn-out. Cords from **appliances** or **extension cords** can also be damaged if they are placed under carpets or furniture. If this happens, then the wires carrying the electricity will show through. This can be very dangerous. You can easily get a bad shock from these wires. Check all your cords every so often for damage. Replace or repair any of them that are worn-out.

Gas in the Home

Some things we have in our homes are run by gas. Three of the most common are stoves, room heaters, and water heaters. These gas appliances can be very useful. But they can also be dangerous. Leaking gas from an appliance can explode. Or, you can die from breathing too much of it. So it's important to follow some guides when using anything in your house that is run by gas.

Gas Leaks

Some gas leaks can be smelled right away. When a pilot light on a stove or heater has gone out, you can always smell gas. Never re-light a pilot light when there is a chance that some gas is in the air. Many heaters have directions for re-lighting a pilot light. Read them carefully.

Never turn on a stove burner or oven and then try to re-light the pilot light. You might have an explosion. Always make sure the knobs on the stove and oven are *turned off*.

Sometimes you may have a gas leak that you can't smell. Carbon monoxide can't be seen or smelled. A gas space heater that is not working properly can leak carbon monoxide. Breathing a certain amount of carbon monoxide for even a short time can kill you.

Electricity and Gas in the Home 55

When relighting the pilot light of a gas stove, always make sure all knobs for the stove and oven are turned *off*.

Don't Take Chances

If you own any gas appliances, always follow these rules.

1. Make sure air gets into your house. Leave a window open at night.

2. If you notice any leaks, shut off the gas line. Don't try to fix the problem yourself. Call someone from the gas company.

3. Have your gas appliances checked once a year for safety.

Special Note:

Remember the dangers of flammable liquids you read about in Chapter 7. Keep all these liquids *far away* from any appliance run by gas. The vapors can cause an explosion and fire.

Gas and electricity help make our lives enjoyable and comfortable. We have become very used to all the things they do for us. And sometimes that means we become careless when using them. Don't be a careless person. Remember the safety rules in this chapter. They can save your home—and your life, too.

Exercises

Darken the circle next to the right answer.

1. Using too many things at one time on an electrical system is called _____ .
   - ○ fusing
   - ○ overloading
   - ○ wiring
   - ○ wattage

2. One way to learn about your home electrical system is by _____ .
   - ○ watching television
   - ○ asking your neighbor
   - ○ calling an electrician to your house
   - ○ taking the system apart

3. As a safety feature, overloaded electrical systems blow fuses or open _____ .
   - ○ hatches
   - ○ locks
   - ○ circuit breakers
   - ○ lightbulbs

4. Using a fuse that is rated too high can cause _____ .
   - ○ an electrical fire
   - ○ a storm
   - ○ a wall to fall
   - ○ all your lights to stay on

5. If your lamps and lights *do not* suggest a certain kind of lightbulb, don't use any _____ .
   - ○ over 100 watts
   - ○ over 60 watts
   - ○ at all
   - ○ under 100 watts

6. If electrical cords become worn-out you should _____ .
   - ○ use them anyway
   - ○ throw out the appliance
   - ○ replace or repair them
   - ○ put them on another appliance

7. Gas leaks are dangerous because they can cause _____ .
   - ○ a flood
   - ○ an explosion
   - ○ windows to break
   - ○ a shock

8. All flammable liquids should be kept far away from gas appliances because _____ .
   - ○ they may dry up
   - ○ they may spoil
   - ○ they may turn hard
   - ○ their vapors could cause an explosion and fire

Words to Remember

| appliances | electrician | extension cords | system |
| capacity | | | |

Posttest

Darken the circle next to the right answer.

1. The first step to take with an open wound that is bleeding badly is to _____ .
   - ○ wash the wound
   - ○ put ice on the wound
   - ○ apply direct pressure to stop the bleeding
   - ○ have the person lie down

2. Sometimes a serious closed wound may be hard to spot because _____ .
   - ○ the victim won't tell you about it
   - ○ you can't see any bleeding
   - ○ the victim could be hungry
   - ○ only doctors can spot closed wounds

3. When a person is in shock, it is important to keep the victim _____ .
   - ○ lying down and covered
   - ○ sitting up in a cool place
   - ○ wide awake at all times
   - ○ in a room all alone

4. In a respiratory emergency, you might use a method of first aid called _____ .
   - ○ choking
   - ○ artificial respiration
   - ○ push-ups
   - ○ knee bends

5. The first *two* steps to take for a poisoning victim are to dilute the poison and _____ .
   - ○ give the person a sleeping pill
   - ○ give the victim food
   - ○ call the Poison Control Center
   - ○ throw the poison away

6. If a poisoning victim is unconscious, you should *not* _____ .
   - ○ loosen any tight clothing around the person's neck and waist
   - ○ give the victim any fluids
   - ○ call for help from a hospital
   - ○ clear an airway for mouth-to-mouth breathing

7. Heat burns are grouped by degree, and the most dangerous burns are _____ .
   - ○ first-degree
   - ○ second-degree
   - ○ third-degree
   - ○ fourth-degree

8. When a person suffers a bad eye burn, *before* calling for medical help you should _____ .
   - ○ bandage the eye
   - ○ wash the eye with large amounts of cool water
   - ○ keep the eye closed for five minutes
   - ○ give the victim a cool drink

9. The condition where parts of the body become frozen is known as _____ .
   - ○ frostbite
   - ○ heartburn
   - ○ a chill
   - ○ heatstroke

10. Two major fire hazards around the house are _____ .
    - ○ food and drinks
    - ○ books and tools
    - ○ flammable liquids and fabrics
    - ○ pots and pans

11. Fabrics that are made so that they are very good at fighting off flames are called _____ .
    - ○ flammable
    - ○ flame resistant
    - ○ upholstery
    - ○ drip-dry

12. Overloading a home electrical system can cause _____ .
    - ○ a power blackout
    - ○ all the lights to stay on
    - ○ the windows to break
    - ○ a flood

Answers to Exercises

Chapter 1
1. wash the wound thoroughly
2. apply a pressure bandage
3. raise the arm or leg above the person's heart
4. removed with a sterilized needle
5. press gently around the edges of the wound
6. place cold compresses on the area
7. very high fever
8. giving the person a tall glass of cold water

Chapter 2
1. traumatic shock
2. rapid and weak pulse; pale and cold skin; shallow and uneven breathing
3. unconsciousness; victim becomes unresponsive; eyes vacant, pupils dilated
4. body temperature will fall
5. depend upon the kind of injury
6. lifted at the feet about 8–12 inches
7. a salt-soda solution
8. four ounces

Chapter 3
1. mouth-to-mouth breathing
2. put person in the right position; clear an airway
3. about every five seconds
4. cover mouth and give mouth-to-nose breathing
5. let the person try to cough out object without help
6. behind the victim with your arms around the person's waist
7. the abdomen
8. lying down, face up

Chapter 4
1. burns around the lips and mouth; strong breath odor
2. dilute the poison; keep the person breathing; get help from a Poison Control Center
3. place your finger in back of the victim's throat; give the person Syrup of Ipecac
4. bleach; liquid cleaner; lighter fluid
5. loosen any tight clothing around the neck and waist; clear an airway for mouth-to-mouth breathing
6. pull the victim out into fresh air; give the victim mouth-to-mouth breathing

Chapter 5
1. third degree
2. put burn under cold running water or cold compress; cover with a clean bandage
3. deep sunburn; touching hot liquids; flash burns
4. 15 percent for an adult, 10 percent for a child
5. skin destroyed; white or charred burn; no pain
6. they go into shock
7. wash with running water for at least five minutes
8. so the chemical will not flow into the other eye

Chapter 6
1. become frozen
2. white, firm skin; very cold, numb skin
3. no higher than 104° Fahrenheit
4. heatstroke
5. cool the victim's body immediately
6. has a normal or slightly higher body temperature and sweats a lot
7. cool water mixed with salt

Chapter 7
1. matches, lighters, pilot lights, or overloaded electrical cords
2. Any three of the following: nail polish remover; paint thinner; gasoline; cleaning fluids
3. True
4. False
5. False
6. False
7. True
8. True

Chapter 8
1. overloading
2. calling an electrician to your house
3. circuit breakers
4. an electrical fire
5. over 60 watts
6. replace or repair them
7. an explosion
8. their vapors could cause an explosion and fire

Posttest
1. apply direct pressure to stop the bleeding
2. you can't see any bleeding
3. lying down and covered
4. artificial respiration
5. call the Poison Control Center
6. give the victim any fluids
7. third-degree
8. wash the eye with large amounts of cool water
9. frostbite
10. flammable liquids and fabrics
11. flame resistant
12. a power blackout